Important note for users of this courseware:

This course is accompanied by additional course documents that can be downloaded for free. Once you have purchased the courseware, please contact the author below for a zip folder containing these files:

E-mail: ProfSkipLaratonda@gmail.com

Allegheny Valley Institute of Technology ®

Authorized Training Programs

About the author:

E. F. Laratonda has over forty years of experience related to analog and digital electrical design, computer and microprocessor-based product design, computer networking, information technology management and computer technology training. His career includes tenures with Texas Instruments, United Technologies, Westinghouse and the Pennsylvania State University. He has managed the design, configuration and administration of hundreds of client computers in both corporate and school district environments and has taught at both the community college and university levels. Presently, he teaches Electrical Engineering at Penn State and helps educate corporate "information technology" personnel in the areas of computer networking, security, operating systems and project management.

E. F. "Skip" Laratonda, MSEE, PE
Director/CEO, Allegheny Valley Institute
Microsoft Certified Systems Engineer
Microsoft Certified Trainer

Allegheny Valley Institute of Technology ®

Authorized Training Programs

Information in this document is subject to change without notice and does not represent a commitment on the part of **Allegheny Valley Institute of Technology**. Under the copyright laws, no part of this document may be copied, photocopied, reproduced, translated, or reduced to any electronic medium or machine-readable form, in whole or in part, without prior written consent of the **Allegheny Valley Institute of Technology**.

Companies, names, and data used in examples herein are fictitious and any similarities are purely coincidental.

ISBN-13:
978-1725536715

ISBN-10:
1725536714

Allegheny Valley Institute of Technology ®

Authorized Training Programs

TABLE OF CONTENTS
VISUAL BASIC FOR APPLICATIONS
LEVEL 2

Allegheny Valley Institute of Technology ®
Authorized Training Programs

Allegheny Valley Institute of Technology ®

Authorized Training Programs

Visual Basic for Applications
Level 2

Working with Additional Properties and Controls

The **Scroll** bar, **Option** button and **CheckBox** are very popular control objects in Windows programs. Using these objects enables the user to select a value by positioning the scroll box to a desired position or clicking the mouse, instead of typing a desired value.

Before we begin your first exercise, create a directory that you will use to save your program files during the course of this class:

   Create a folder called **"VBA Class"** on your desktop.

Allegheny Valley Institute of Technology ®

Authorized Training Programs

The Temperature Conversion Program

The follow exercise will introduce you to additional controls and help to demonstrate other useful programming techniques.

Exercise #1 Specification:

Write a Visual Basic program called **TEMPERATURE** that will display the following window when started:

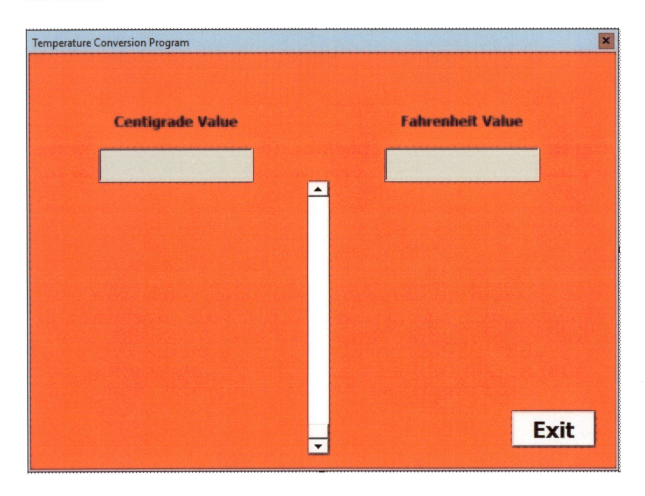

The window will be comprised of two labels, two text boxes, one vertical scroll bar and one button, as shown above. When you change the scroll box of the scroll bar, the left text box will display a temperature in degrees Centigrade. The right text box will show the equivalent temperature in degrees Fahrenheit. When you click on the **Exit** button, the program will terminate.

Allegheny Valley Institute of Technology ®

Authorized Training Programs

The Visual Programming of the TEMPERATURE Program
Creating the UserForm

Use the following steps to create a new project file for the **Name** program:

1. Start **Excel** and open a blank workbook.

2. Under the **Developer** tab in the **Code** group, click the **Visual Basic** button and the **Microsoft Visual Basic Editor** window will appear.

3. On the **Menu,** click **Insert** and choose **UserForm**.

   Re-arrange and re-size the windows to look like:

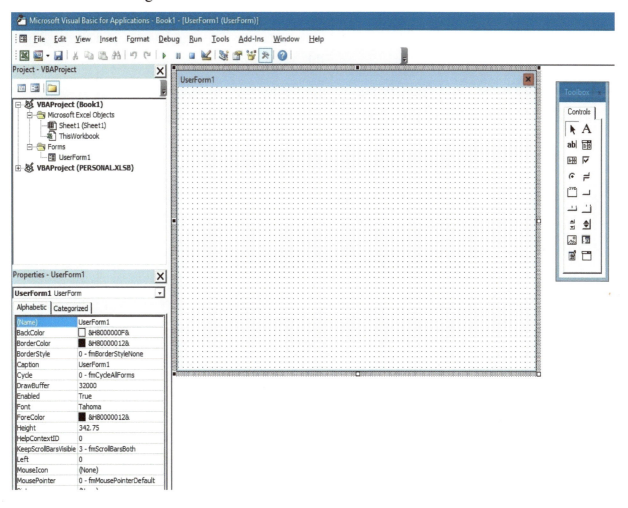

Allegheny Valley Institute of Technology ®
Authorized Training Programs

Build the **frmMain** form from the following **Properties Table**.

The completed form should look like the one shown in the specification on page 2.

Make sure you *check off* the setting after you have entered it from the table.

Object	Property	Property Setting
Form	**Name**	**frmTemp**
	Caption	Temperature Conversion Program
	BackColor	(make it red)
	Height	370
	Width	508
Label	**Name**	**lblCentigrade**
	TextAlign	2-Center
	BackColor	(make it red)
	Caption	Centigrade Value
	Font	Bold, 12 point
	Height	25
	Left	60
	Top	50
	Width	132
Label	**Name**	**lblFahrenheit**
	TextAlign	2-Center
	BackColor	(make it red)
	Caption	Fahrenheit Value
	Font	Bold, 12 point
	Height	25
	Left	306
	Top	50
	Width	132

Allegheny Valley Institute of Technology ®

Authorized Training Programs

Text Box	Name	txtCentigrade
	TextAlign	2-Center
	BackColor	(make it light gray)
	ForeColor	(make it blue)
	Height	28
	Left	60
	Top	80
	Width	132
	Text	(none)
	Font	18
Text Box	Name	txtFahrenheit
	TextAlign	2-Center
	BackColor	(make it light gray)
	ForeColor	(make it blue)
	Height	28
	Left	306
	Top	80
	Width	132
	Text	(none)
	Font	18
Vertical Scroll Bar	Name	vsbTemp
	Height	228
	Left	240
	Large Change	10
	Max	100
	Min	-40
	Top	108
	Value	-40
	Width	18

Allegheny Valley Institute of Technology ®

Authorized Training Programs

Command Button	Name	cmdExit	
	Caption	Exit	
	Font	Bold 18 pt	
	Height	30	See note below
	Left	415	See note below
	Top	300	See note below
	Width	70	See note below

Note: The values of height, left, top and width are measured in **points** (there are 72 points in an inch).

Therefore:

    36 points = ½ inch

    18 points = ¼ inch

Additional Properties (Left, Top, Height and Width)

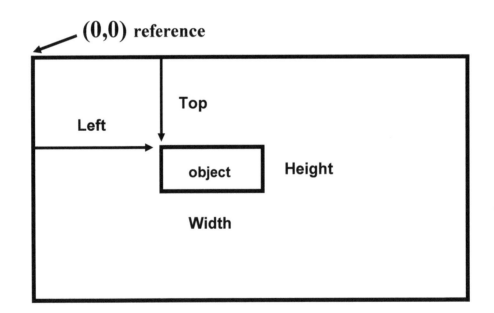

Allegheny Valley Institute of Technology ®

Authorized Training Programs

Save Your Work!

Select **File/Save** and the following message will appear:

You must click **NO** to the following message!

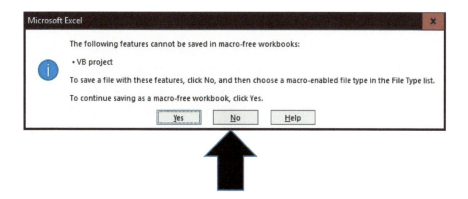

Because the workbook has a macro embedded in it, you must save it as an **Excel Macro-Enabled Workbook**.

Select **File/Save** again and save the workbook in the **VBA Class** folder on the desktop as **TEMPERATURE** but this time as an:

Excel Macro-Enabled Workbook

Allegheny Valley Institute of Technology ®

Authorized Training Programs

Entering the Code for the TEMPERATURE Program

1. Double-click on the **Exit** button.

2. After the Sub statement, type **End**

3. Select **File/Save** from the **Menu** bar.

Although you did not complete writing the code of the TEMPERATURE program yet, execute the TEMP program to see what you have accomplished so far:

1. To execute the TEMPERATURE program, you may press **F5**, or select **Run** from the **Menu** bar, or click the **Run** icon on the tool bar.

2. Change the scroll bar position by clicking the up and down arrows of the scroll bar. As you can see nothing is happening, because you did not attach any code to the scroll bar.

3. Click the **Exit** button to terminate the program.

The Min, Max, and Value Properties of the Vertical Scroll Bar

A scroll bar represents a set of values. The *Maximum* and *Minimum* properties represent the range of values that can be selected by the scroll bar. The *Value* property represents the value that is displayed when the program is first executed.

Allegheny Valley Institute of Technology ®

Authorized Training Programs

Review of Assigning Values to the Properties of Objects

Syntax:

ObjectName. Property = Value

Entering Code for the Vertical Scroll Bar

1. Double-click on the vertical scroll bar.
2. Enter the code: **txtCentigrade.Text = vsbTemp.Value & " C"**

Execute the Program and notice that it has three minor problems:

- You can type in the text boxes. This is not good!!
- When you move the scroll box the value does not update until you release the mouse button. This is not good!!
- The value is not being converted to degrees Fahrenheit. This is not good!!

Enter the additional properties and code to correct these problems:

3. Display the **Property List** for each **Text Box** and change the *Locked* property to **True**.

4. Enter the following code inside the vsbTemp_Scroll() procedure:

   <u>Make sure you select the Scroll procedure as the event!</u>

   txtCentigrade.Text = vsbTemp.Value & " C"

Notice that this code is identical to the code inside the vsbTemp_Change() procedure.

Entering the Conversion Code

Enter the following code in both the **vsbTemp_Change ( )** procedure and the **vsbTemp_Scroll ( )** procedure:

```
Private Sub vsbTemp_Change()

    Dim CentValue As Integer

    Dim FahrValue As Single


    txtCentigrade.Text = vsbTemp.Value & " C"        'display Centigrade value

    CentValue = vsbTemp.Value                         'load Centigrade variable

    FahrValue = 9 / 5 * CentValue + 32                'load Fahrenheit variable

    txtFahrenheit.Text = FahrValue & " F"             'display Fahrenheit value

End Sub
```

The TEMPERATURE program demonstrated how you can create a friendly, graphical user interface for entering numbers.

On the next few pages, we are going to discuss **Flow Charting** and use "If Statements" to modify the **TEMPERATURE** program.

Before we begin, let's see how we can control VBA code by using **If** Statements.

Allegheny Valley Institute of Technology ®

Authorized Training Programs

Flow Charting

A *flowchart* is a type of diagram that represents an algorithm, workflow or process, showing the steps as boxes of various kinds, and their order by connecting them with arrows. It is an intermediate step between the conceptual algorithm and the actual writing of the program code.

(See page 37 of Level 1 course notes.)

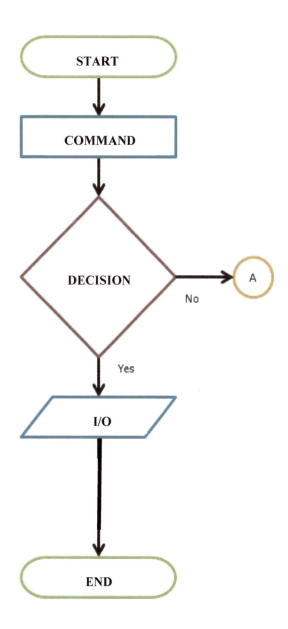

Allegheny Valley Institute of Technology ®

Authorized Training Programs

Modifying the original Temperature specification:

Write the additional code necessary to change the **ForeColor** of both text boxes to **red** and "beep" when the centigrade value is greater than or equal to 95°C.

Code:

How could you modify the code to <u>also change</u> the **ForeColor** of both text boxes to **green** and "beep" when the centigrade value is less than or equal to -35°C?

Code:

Allegheny Valley Institute of Technology ®

Authorized Training Programs

Making Decisions with Visual Basic Code

As you write the code you can, create procedures that make decisions based on certain conditions. The two basic types of decision statements are *If* statements and *Select Case* statements. The other major type of control statement is the *loop*.

You use *loops* (the running of several statements repeatedly to achieve a desired result) to perform repetitive tasks in your program.

Making Decisions with If Statements

There are three types of **If statements** that can be used to make decisions in your VBA programs:

- **If ... Then**
- **If...Then ... Else**
- **If...Then ... ElseIf**

Using If...Then Statements to Make Decisions

These statements makes decisions and can only have two consequences (*True* or *False*). Use the **If...Then** statement to test for simple TRUE/FALSE conditions such as:

If *Temperature >= 95* **Then** GoTo *Alert*

If...Then Statements use the following two syntaxes:

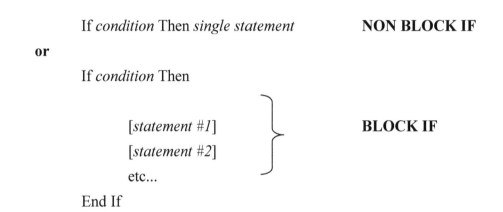

or

If *condition* Then *single statement*   **NON BLOCK IF**

If *condition* Then

> [*statement #1*]
> [*statement #2*]
> etc...

End If   **BLOCK IF**

condition	You can use either a logical expression that returns True or False, or you can use any expression that returns a numeric value. If the expression returns a numeric value, a return value of zero is functionally equivalent as False, and any nonzero value is equivalent to True.
statement(s)	* The **VBA** statement(s) to run if the condition returns True. If the condition returns False, **Visual Basic** skips over the statements.

* The *statement(s)* can be text strings, calculations and/or branch operations such as **GOTO.**

Whether you use the single-line or block syntax depends on the number of statements you want to run if the condition returns a True value.

Allegheny Valley Institute of Technology ®
Authorized Training Programs

Using If...Then...Else Statements to Make Decisions

Using the **If...Then** statement to make decisions in your code adds a powerful command when programming in **Visual Basic**. However, this command has a major drawback: a *False* result only avoids one or more statements; it doesn't execute any of its own. This is fine in many cases, but there will be times when you need to run one group of statements if the condition returns *True* and a different group if the result is *False*. The **If...Then...Else** statement will handle this:

If...Then...Else Statements use the following syntax:

If *condition* Then

[*TrueStatements*]

Else

[*FalseStatements*]

End If

condition	You can use either a logical expression that returns True or False, or you can use any expression that returns a numeric value.
	If the expression returns a numeric value, a return value of zero is functionally equivalent as False, and any nonzero value is equivalent to True.
TrueStatements	The **VBA** statement(s) to run if the condition returns *True*.
FalseStatements	The **VBA** statement(s) to run if the condition returns *False*.

Allegheny Valley Institute of Technology ®

Authorized Training Programs

Working with Multiple If Statements

In the preceding pages, you saw the simple block **If** statements, which evaluate one condition and can execute commands for either a *True* or a *False* condition. You can also evaluate multiple conditions with an additional statement in the block **If** format. The **ElseIf** statement will handle this:

ElseIf Statements use the following syntax:

> If *1st condition* Then
>> [*TrueStatements*]
>
> ElseIf *2nd condition* Then
>> [*TrueStatements*]
>
> Else
>> [*FalseStatements*]
>
> End If

This format can continue for as many **ElseIf** statements as you require.

condition	You can use either a logical expression that returns True or False, or you can use any expression that returns a numeric value. If the expression returns a numeric value, a return value of zero is functionally equivalent as False, and any nonzero value is equivalent to True.
TrueStatements	The **VBA** statement(s) to run if the condition returns *True*.
FalseStatements	The **VBA** statement(s) to run if the condition returns *False*.

Allegheny Valley Institute of Technology ®
Authorized Training Programs

Using Select Case Statements to Make Multiple Decisions

The problem with *If...* statements is that normally you can make only a single decision. The statement calculates a single logical result and performs one of two actions. The block *Select Case* statement is a powerful command in **Visual Basic** that enables the programmer to make multiple decisions that don't fit into *True* or *False* categories. A *Select Case* statement can test for many conditions until it finds a condition that is *True*. When *If* finds a *True* condition, then it runs the statement(s) within that section of the code.

The *Select Case* statement consists of multiple sub-statements, each on different lines of Visual Basic code.

Select Case Statements use the following syntax:

Select Case *TestExpression*

Case1 *FirstExpressionList*
[*FirstStatements*]
Case2 *SecondExpressionList*
[*SecondStatements*]...

Case Else
[ElseStatements]
End Select

TestExpression	* See **VBA** Help
ExpressionList	* See **VBA** Help
Statements	* See **VBA** Help

Allegheny Valley Institute of Technology ®

Authorized Training Programs

Using Dialog Boxes

A **dialog box** is a window used to display and/or accept information. Its name comes from the fact that it is, in essence, a ***dialog*** (or conversation) with the user. We will look at two dialog boxes built into **Visual Basic**:

- The Message Box
- The Input Box

Displaying and Getting Information with the Message Box

A well designed application is one that keeps the user involved. It should display messages at appropriate times and ask the user for input. When interacting with the application, the user feels that he or she is a part of the process and has control over the program. You can use the **MessageBox** to display messages to the user and to get the user's response to Yes/No type of questions.

Displaying a Message Using the MsgBox Statement

When the user needs to see a message, you can use the ***MsgBox*** statement:

MsgBox "Message", DialogType, "Title"

Message	The message you want to display in the dialog box
DialogType	A number or constant that specifies, among other things, the command buttons that appear in the dialog (See the next page.) The default value is 0.
Title	The text that appears in the dialog box title bar. If you omit title, **Visual Basic** uses the project's name.

Button Constants

Constant Name	Value	Displayed Buttons
vbOKOnly	0	OK
vbOKCancel	1	OK, Cancel
vbAbortRetryIgnore	2	Abort, Retry, Ignore
vbYesNoCancel	3	Yes, No, Cancel
vbYesNo	4	Yes, No
vbRetryCancel	5	Retry, Cancel

Icon Constants

Constant Name	Value	Displayed Icon
vbCritical	16	The Stop Sign icon
vbQuestion	32	The Question Mark icon
vbExclamation	48	The Exclamation icon
vbInformation	64	The Information icon

Modal Constants

Constant Name	Value	Displayed Icon
vbApplicationModal	0	Forces the user to provide an answer before continuing to use Excel.
vbSystemModal	4096	Forces the user to provide an answer before continuing to use any program on the computer. (dialog box in foreground)

Note: UserForms can be either Modal or Modeless

Allegheny Valley Institute of Technology ®

Authorized Training Programs

Exercise #2: By clicking a **CommandButton** on a **UserForm**, create the following **Message Boxes**:

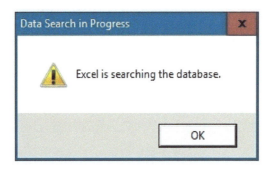

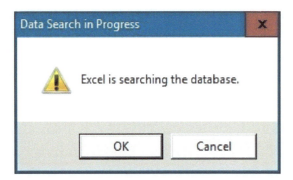

Using the Message Box with Variables

' This is a simple message box test

```
Private Sub cmdMessage_Click ()
    Dim Message As String
    Dim DialogType As Integer
    Dim Title As String

    ' The message of the dialog box.
    Message = "This can be very useful!"

    ' The dialog box should have an OK button and
    ' an exclamation icon.
    DialogType = VbOKOnly + VbExclamation

    ' The title of the dialog box.
    Title = "Dialog Box Demonstration"

    ' Display the dialog box.
    MsgBox   Message,  DialogType,  Title
End Sub
```

Creating "Line Breaks" in Dialog Boxes

For long prompts, **Visual Basic** wraps the text inside the dialog box. If you would like to create your own line breaks, use the **Chr** function and the carriage-return character (ASCII 13) between each line:

MsgBox "First line" & Chr (13) & "Second line"

or in place of the Chr(13) you can use **VbCr**

Allegheny Valley Institute of Technology ®

Authorized Training Programs

Modal and Modeless Dialog Boxes and UserForms

Most **Dialog Boxes** and **UserForms** that you encounter are *modal*, which means you must dismiss the **Dialog Box** on the screen or the **UserForm** before the user can do anything with the underlying application. In some cases, you may want to make the **Dialog Box** or **UserForm** modeless which will allow you to work with the underlying application while the **Dialog Box** or **UserForm** is displayed.

By default, **Dialog Boxes** and **UserForms** are **modal**.

To display a **modeless UserForm**, use a statement such as:

- frmMain.Show vbModeless

or

- frmMain.Show 0

Exercise: Creating a Modeless UserForm

To test this, open **Temperature** and place a button from the top left of cell H2 to the bottom right of cell I3. Then create a **New** macro called "Start_Click" which will simply show the UserForm:

    frmMain.Show

Wait for the instructor.

Allegheny Valley Institute of Technology ®

Authorized Training Programs

Getting Return Values Using the MsgBox Function

When the program code needs to use the returned value of the **Message Box**, you can also use the **MsgBox** function:

$$VariableName = MsgBox \text{ (“Message”, DialogType, “Title”)}$$

The returned value of the **MsgBox( )** function indicates which button in the dialog box was clicked by the user:

The Output Constants of the **MsgBox ( ) Function**

Constant Name	Value	Clicked Button
VbOK	1	**OK** button was clicked
VbCancel	2	**Cancel** button was clicked
VbAbort	3	**Abort** button was clicked
VbRetry	4	**Retry** button was clicked
VbIgnore	5	**Ignore** button was clicked
VbYes	6	**Yes** button was clicked
VbNo	7	**No** button was clicked

Note: The **MsgBox**, like all **Visual Basic** functions, needs parentheses around its arguments only when the function's return value is to be used. This is the only difference between the **MsgBox Statement** and **MsgBox Function**.

If you need to determine which button the user clicked, the value of the *variable* assigned to the *return value* must be examined with *If statements*. The following exercise will demonstrate.

Allegheny Valley Institute of Technology ®

Authorized Training Programs

Using the "Return Values" in a Message Box Function

Exercise #3: Create the following **Form** and **Message Box**:

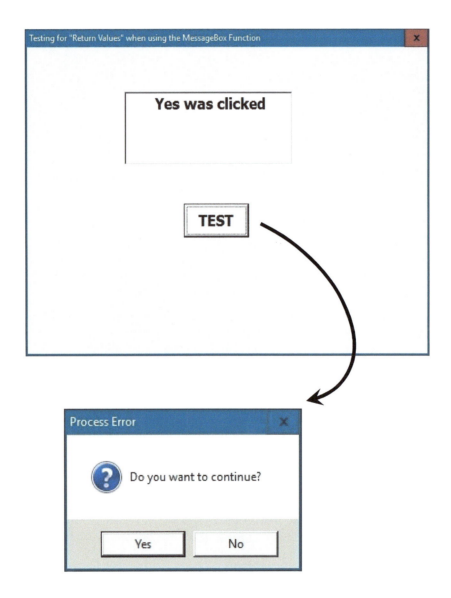

Allegheny Valley Institute of Technology ®

Authorized Training Programs

The cmdTest( )_Click code:

```
Private Sub cmdTest_Click()
    Dim ReturnValue As Integer

    ReturnValue = MsgBox("Do you want to continue?", 36, "Process Error")
    If ReturnValue = 6 Then
        txtBox.Text = "Yes was clicked"
        Else
        txtBox.Text = "No was clicked"
    End If
End Sub
```

Modify the Temperature specification:

Exercise #4

Write the additional code necessary to display the following **MessageBox** when the temperature reaches 95 degrees centigrade.

(Reference pages 18 and 19)

Code:

Allegheny Valley Institute of Technology ®

Authorized Training Programs

Getting Input Using the InputBox Function

As you've seen, the **MsgBox** function enables your procedures to interact with the user and get some feedback. Unfortunately, this method limits you to simple command button responses. For more varied user input, you need to use more sophisticated techniques.

Prompting the User for Input

The **InputBox** function displays a dialog box with a message that prompts the user to enter data, and it provides an edit box for the data itself. The syntax for this method appears as the following:

$$VariableName = InputBox (``prompt", ``title", ``default", xpos, ypos)$$

prompt	The message you want to display in the dialog box.
title	The text that appears in the dialog box title bar. The default value is the null string (nothing).
default	The default value displayed in the edit box. If you omit default, the edit box is displayed empty. (optional)
xpos	The horizontal position of the dialog box from the left edge of the screen. The value is measured in twips or twentieths of a point. (there are 1440 twips in an inch). If you omit xpos, the dialog box is centered horizontally. (optional)
ypos	The vertical position, in twips, from the top of the screen. If you omit ypos, the dialog is centered vertically in the current window. (optional)

Allegheny Valley Institute of Technology ®

Authorized Training Programs

Using the Input Box Function

Exercise #5: Create the following **UserForm** and **Input Boxes:**

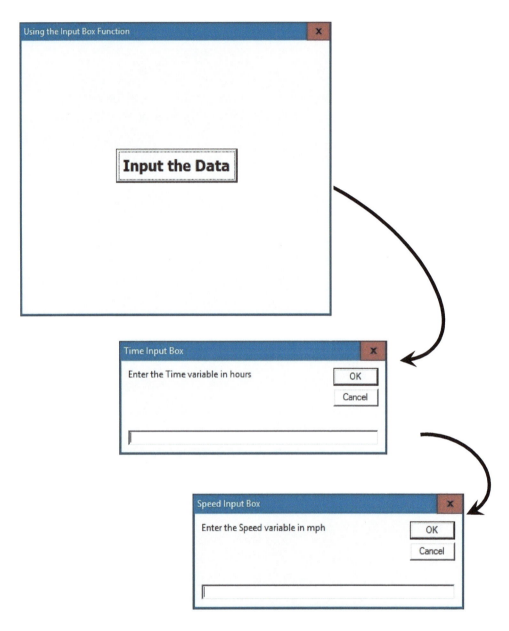

The code for the *click* procedure of the **command** button is on the next page.

Allegheny Valley Institute of Technology ®

Authorized Training Programs

The **cmdInput( )_Click** code:

Private Sub cmdInput_Click( )
   Dim Time1 **As** Single
   Dim Speed1 **As** Single
   Dim Distance **As** Double

   Time1 = **InputBox**("Enter the Time variable in hours", "Time Input Box", "")
   Speed1 = **InputBox**("Enter the Speed variable in mph", "Speed Input Box", "")
   Distance = Time1 * Speed1
   MsgBox "Distance = " & Distance & " miles", 0, "Distance Calculator"

End Sub

       The **InputBox** function returns one of the following values:

          *   The value entered into the edit box, if the user clicks on **OK**.
          *   An empty string, if the user clicks on **Cancel**.

   You store the result by assigning a variable to the ***InputBox*** statement. You can then use this variable to test the result (with *If...Then...Else* or *Select Case*). or you can use the variable in other statements and calculations.

- Execute your program with all variables **Dimmed** As **Byte, Integer and Single** and notice if there are any issues! Why are there? (see page 41 of Level 1)

- Execute your program without entering data in either of the **Input Boxes** and notice if there are any issues! Why are there?

- Execute your program and enter text in either of the **Input Boxes** and notice if there are any issues! Why are there?

Introduction to Error Trapping

The importance of code running correctly cannot be overstated. If an error occurs in an event procedure and you code does not handle it, the control will *crash* and the end-user will most likely become confused. Users are depending on you to create a product that they can use with confidence.

How can we improve the previous program from an "Error-Handling" point of view?

Notes:

Notes:

Allegheny Valley Institute of Technology ®

Authorized Training Programs

Converting Inches to Centimeters (Homework)

' This macro will convert inches to centimeters using the **InputBox** function.

```
Private Sub cmdConvertTest_Click ()
        Dim MyNumber As Single
        Dim Answer As Single
        Const Multiplier = 2.54


        MyNumber  =  InputBox ("Enter a value in inches", _
        "Converting Inches to Centimeters")


        'Check for a valid input
         If  MyNumber < 0 Then
                MsgBox  "Your input number is not valid!", 16, "Conversion
                Failed"
        Else
                Answer = MyNumber * Multiplier
                MsgBox "Your answer is" & Chr(13) & Answer _
                        & " centimeters", , "Conversion Exercise"
        End If

    End Sub
```

Note: Enter the necessary code to trap all data entry errors.

Allegheny Valley Institute of Technology ®

Authorized Training Programs

Debugging Visual Basic Macro Code

In **Excel**, macros are written in a language called **Visual Basic for Applications**, or **VBA**.

When you write a macro, you need to test it and correct any errors in the macro. This process is called **debugging**. The process of debugging a macro in **VBA** is the same as debugging in any other programming language. All you need to do is step through the macro, one command at a time, and make sure it works as you think it should. You do this by viewing both the windows for your macro and a test worksheet. As you step through the macro (using the commands available in the **Debug** menu of the **VBA Editor**), you can correct any errors you locate.

Useful Tools for Debugging a Macro

Debugging a program is one of the most important steps in software development. Knowledge of **VBA's** debugging tools can make debugging easier and more productive. This page describes several of **VBA's** built-in debugging tools you can use when testing and debugging your application.

- Command Stepping
- Breakpoints and the Stop command
- Local Windows
- Immediate Window

Command Stepping

One of the first methods to **debug code** is to step through the code one line at a time.

To step through code, put the cursor on the first line of code to be analyzed and press **F8** or choose **Step Into** on the **Debug** menu. The next line of code to be executed will be displayed in yellow background with a black font. Note that the highlighted line of code has not yet been executed -- it is the next line to execute.

If your code calls another procedure, stepping through the code with **F8** will cause execution to enter the called procedure in a line-by-line sequence. If you want to execute the called procedure without stepping through it, press **SHIFT F8**. This will execute the called procedure and then pause on the line of code after calling the procedure. If you are already stepping through a procedure, you can press **CTRL F8** to resume code execution line-by-line. At any time you are paused either in step-by-step mode or at a breakpoint (see below), you can press **F5** or *Continue* from the **Run** menu to cause **VBA** to run to completion or until a pause statement is encountered.

Whenever you are paused in step-by-step mode, you can query or change a variable's value from the **Immediate window**.

Allegheny Valley Institute of Technology ®

Authorized Training Programs

Breakpoints and the Stop command

A **breakpoint** is a marker placed on a line of code that causes execution to pause immediately before executing that line. You can add a **breakpoint** to a line of code by putting the cursor on the line of code in question and pressing **F9**, choosing *Toggle Breakpoint* on the **Debug** menu, or clicking in the left margin next to the line of code. When a **breakpoint** is set, the line is displayed in brick-red background with a white font. When you run the code, execution will pause immediately before the line of code with the breakpoint and will display it in yellow background with a black font. Note than the line in yellow has not yet been executed -- it is the next line of code to run.

While the code is paused at the **breakpoint**, you can issue commands in the **Immediate window** to change or query a variable's value. To view the content of a variable, enter a **?** character followed by the name of the variable and then press **ENTER**. You can change a variable's value by entering *VariableName = NewValue* in the Immediate window and pressing **ENTER**.

If the **Immediate window** is not visible (typically at the bottom of the **VBA Editor** screen), press **CTRL G** or choose *Immediate Window* from the **View** menu to make the window visible.

To remove a breakpoint, put the cursor on the line of code and press **F9**. You can clear all breakpoints by choosing **Clear All Breakpoints** from the **Debug** menu or pressing **CTRL SHIFT F9**.

VBA also provides the Stop command. This simply stops code execution on that line of code and enters break mode.

Once you are finished debugging the code, be sure to go back and clear all breakpoints (choose *Clear All Breakpoints* from the **Debug** menu or press **CTRL SHIFT F9**) and be sure to remove or comment out all Stop statements.

When you are paused at a breakpoint or in step-by-step mode, you can change the next line to be executed, either before the current line to re-run a section of code, or after the line to skip statements. Right-click the line where you want execution to resume and right-click and choose *Set Next Statement* or choose *Set Next Statement* from the Run menu. Execution will resume at the selected line of code.

Allegheny Valley Institute of Technology ®

Authorized Training Programs

The Locals Window

The **Locals windows** allows you to view the value of all the variables in a procedure when you are stepping through the procedure. To display the **Locals window**, choose **Locals Window** from the **View** menu. Using the **Locals window** is easier to display variable values than examining the value from the **Immediate window**. For simple variable types (e.g., Long and String variables), the value is displayed on one line. For complex types or objects (e.g., a Range variable), its properties are displayed in a collapsible tree-like structure.

Immediate Window

Click Immediate Window on the View Menu or press Ctrl+G. The **Immediate window** is a primary debugging area, and it is used to: (i) display results of debug statements in your macro; (ii) you can type a **vba** statement or a line of code directly into the window and press **Enter** to execute it; and (iii) you can also change the value of a variable while running a macro - when your macro is in break mode and pauses, you can assign a new value to the variable (in the **Immediate window**) as you would in the macro itself. In the **Immediate window** you can evaluate vba statements or expressions which may be related to your macro or unrelated, and whether your macro is running or not.

When your macro is in break mode, a vba statement in the **Immediate Window** is executed in the context of that macro - ex. if you type MsgBox i (where i is a variable name being used in the macro) in the **Immediate window**, you will get the current macro value of the variable i as if this command (MsgBox i) was being executed within the macro. You can now change this current variable value (of i) by assigning a new value to it in the Immediate window, and then continue or test your code with the new assigned value. You will also often type vba commands directly in the Immediate window, to evaluate them.

To return a value, precede the expression with a question mark, ex. **?rownumber**, and omit the question mark to run a code which does not return a value.

Allegheny Valley Institute of Technology ®

Authorized Training Programs

Using Breakpoints to Debug a Macro

A *breakpoint* is a marker placed on a line of code that causes execution to pause immediately before executing that line. You can add a breakpoint to a line of code by putting the cursor on the line of code in question and pressing **F9**, choosing *Toggle Breakpoint* on the **Debug** menu, or <u>clicking in the left margin next to the line of code</u>.

Exercise: Using Breakpoints

1. Open the **Temperature** program and change the initial value of **vsbTemp** to 50.

2. Then add a ***breakpoint*** as shown below:

```
Private Sub vsbTemp_Change()

    txtCentigrade.Text = vsbTemp.Value & "°C"    'Display Centigrade Value
    CentValue = vsbTemp.Value                     'Set Variable Value
    FahrValue = 9 / 5 * CentValue + 32            'Calculate Variable
    txtFahrenheit.Text = FahrValue & "°F"         'Display Value

    'This code will only cancel alert if moving down
    If vsbTemp.Value >= 95 Then
        Beep
        txtCentigrade.ForeColor = vbRed
        txtFahrenheit.ForeColor = vbRed
        If CentValueNew < CentValue Then

            MsgBox "Caution! You are reaching the boiling point", 48, "Ten

        End If
    ElseIf vsbTemp.Value <= -35 Then
        Beep
        txtCentigrade.ForeColor = vbGreen
        txtFahrenheit.ForeColor = vbGreen
    Else
        txtCentigrade.ForeColor = RGB(0, 0, 255)
        txtFahrenheit.ForeColor = RGB(0, 0, 255)
    End If
        CentValueNew = CentValue

End Sub
```

Allegheny Valley Institute of Technology ®

Authorized Training Programs

3. Then run the **Temperature** program and "Change" the temperature value but do not go below -34 degrees until told to do so. Notice the program should "pause" at the breakpoint if you change the vsbTemp control to a value below or equal to -35.

4. While the macro is paused, hover over the code "**vsbTemp.Value**" in the macro just above the breakpoint, to evaluate that code.

5. While the macro is paused type, **?vsbTemp.Value** in the **Immediate window** to evaluate the code.

Allegheny Valley Institute of Technology ®

Authorized Training Programs

Using Loops

Another procedure that involves decisions making is looping. **Visual Basic** allows a procedure to be repeated many times until a condition or a set of conditions is fulfilled. This is generally called *looping*. Looping is a very useful feature of **Visual Basic** because it makes repetitive works easier.

Visual Basic loop structures allow you to run one or more lines of code repetitively. You can repeat the statements in a loop structure until a condition is **True**, until a condition is **False**, a specified number of times, or once for each element in a collection.

The following illustration shows a loop structure that runs a set of statements until a condition becomes true.

Running a set of statements until a condition becomes true

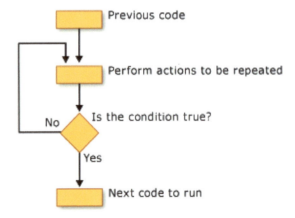

Allegheny Valley Institute of Technology ®

Authorized Training Programs

If, in your VBA program, you need to perform the same task (i.e. repeat the same piece of code) multiple times, this can be done using one of the VBA Loops.

There are two kinds of loops in **VBA**:

1. **Do...Loop**

2. **For.......Next loop**.

The Do ... Loop

The **Do ... Loop** statements have four different forms, as shown below:

1. **Do While** condition

    Block of one or more VB statements

    Loop

2. **Do**

    Block of one or more VB statements

    Loop While condition

3. **Do Until** condition

    Block of one or more VB statements

    Loop

4. **Do**

    Block of one or more VB statements

    Loop Until condition

Allegheny Valley Institute of Technology ®

Authorized Training Programs

Loop Example 1:

```
Sub Example1 ()
    Dim Number As Integer
    Number = 1                          'set initial condition for the Number

    Do While Number < 5
        MsgBox Number
        Number = Number + 1
    Loop
End Sub
```

Loop Example 2:

```
Private Sub cmdStart_Click()
    Dim Counter As Integer
    Counter = 0                         'set initial condition for the Counter

    Do While Counter < = 10
        txtCounter.Text = Counter
        Counter = Counter + 1
    Loop
End Sub
```

* The above example will keep on adding until counter >10.

The above example can be rewritten as:

```
Do
        num.Text = counter
        counter = counter + 1
Loop until counter > 10
```

Allegheny Valley Institute of Technology ®

Authorized Training Programs

The For .... Next Loop

The **For**....**Next Loop** event procedure is written as follows:

For counter = startNumber to endNumber (Step increment)
        One or more VB statements
Next

Loop Example 3:

```
Public Sub DeleteRows()
Dim RowNumber As Integer

For RowNumber = 5 To 14 Step 2
    Rows(RowNumber).Delete
Next RowNumber

End Sub
```

Note: Depending on how you intend to use the **Step**, it can be either a positive or a negative value. See **Loop Example 3.xlsm**

Allegheny Valley Institute of Technology ®

Authorized Training Programs

Using a Form to enter data onto a Worksheet

Exercise #6: Using a UserForm to enter data onto a worksheet

1. Open **Microsoft Excel**

2. Create the following worksheet:

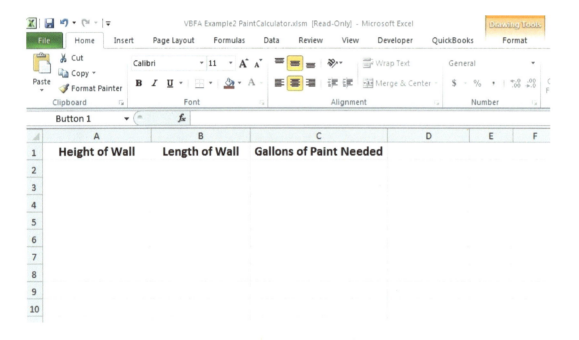

Allegheny Valley Institute of Technology ®

Authorized Training Programs

3. On the **Developer** tab in the **Code** group, click the **Visual Basic** button and the **Microsoft Visual Basic for Applications** window will appear:

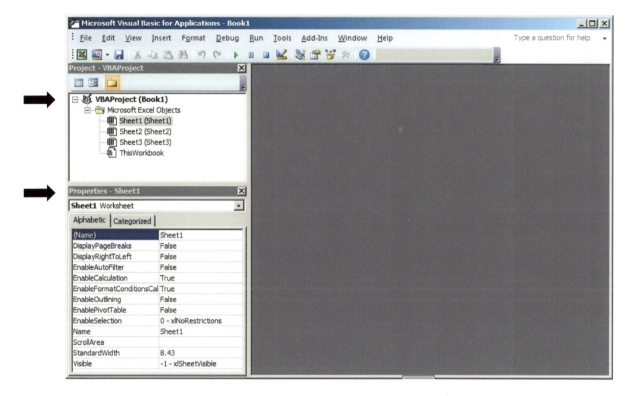

Notice the **Project** and **Properties** windows are on the left side!

Allegheny Valley Institute of Technology ®

Authorized Training Programs

4. On the **Menu,** click **Insert** and choose **UserForm**.

Notice how the interface changes:

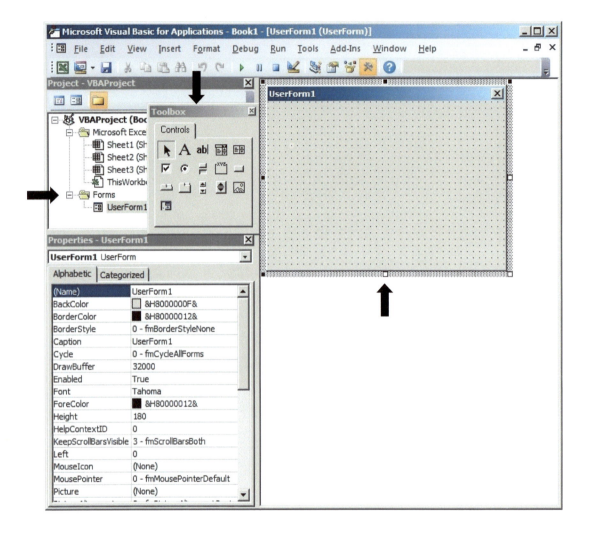

Allegheny Valley Institute of Technology ®

Authorized Training Programs

5. Increase the size of the form slightly by dragging the lower-right handle to the bottom right.

6. Using good naming conventions (starting with the userform) and reasonable properties for all objects, create the user interface shown below:

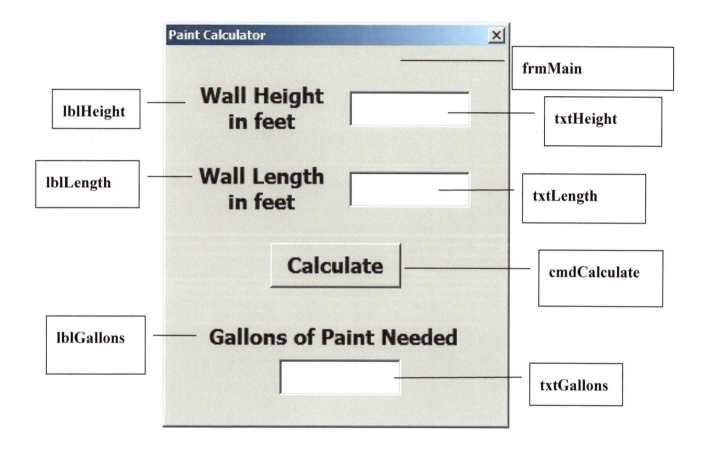

Allegheny Valley Institute of Technology ®

Authorized Training Programs

7. After you create the form, refer below and save it by clicking **File/SaveBook1** and make the following edits:

Filename: Paint Calculator

Save as type: Excel Macro-Enabled Workbook (*.xlsm)

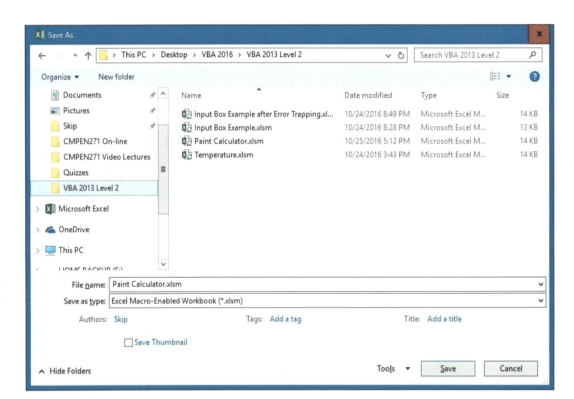

8. Then click the **Save** button. The UserForm will be saved with the workbook called **Paint Calculator.xlsm**

Allegheny Valley Institute of Technology ®

Authorized Training Programs

Entering Visual Basic code Calculate Button

On the **UserForm**, double-click the **Calculate** button and add the following code:

```
Private Sub cmdCalculate_Click( )
    Dim Height As Single
    Dim Length As Single
    Dim Area As Single
    Dim Gallons As Single

    'Calculate the gallons of paint needed
    Height = txtHeight.Value
    Length = txtLength.Value
    Area = Height * Length
    Gallons = Area / 400
    txtGallons.Text = Gallons

    'Place data onto the worksheet
    Range("A2") = Height
    Range("B2") = Length
    Range("C2") = Gallons
End Sub
```

"*Error trap*" the code above using the techniques discussed on page 30 and 31.

Allegheny Valley Institute of Technology ®

Authorized Training Programs

Attaching your form to the Workbook with a Command button

1. View the worksheet by clicking on the **Microsoft Excel** button in the upper left corner or pressing **ALT + F11**

2. On the **Developer** tab in the **Control** group, click the **Insert** button and choose the **Button** control and draw a **command** button between E3 and G6 on the worksheet approximately 2 row by 2 columns in size and when you release the mouse the following dialog box will appear:

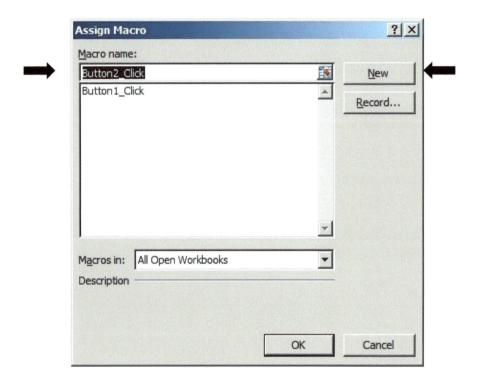

3. Name the macro: **PaintCalculator_Click** and click the **New** button.

4. Type in the code: **frmMain.Show**

5. Highlight the **Button1** text and change it to **Add Dimensions**

Allegheny Valley Institute of Technology ®

Authorized Training Programs

6. You can now "call" the form by just clicking on the **Add Dimensions** button on the worksheet!

7. Save your work!

8. If you need to edit the **Add Dimensions** button, just right-click it!

9. Run the **PaintCalculator** macro

Observation:

What is a major limitation of this application macro?

Add the code necessary to fix this issue using the following **VBA code** *properties*:

- Use the **ActiveCell(row, column)** *property* to select each of the "3" cells instead of the **Range( )** *object*.

- Use the **ActiveCell.Offset** *property* to move down the row.

Note: This exercise <u>does not</u> require using loops but it will require you to Google for help on the following message:
   "Move the active cell by using ActiveCell.Offset"

Allegheny Valley Institute of Technology ®

Authorized Training Programs

The VBA Timer Function

The VBA **Timer Function** returns a **Single** data type, representing the number of seconds that have elapsed since midnight of the current day. (0 to 86,400)

The function takes no arguments and therefore the syntax of the function is simply:

Timer( )

The **Timer Function** produces an output that takes on the format:

XXXXX.XX

Understanding the Timer Function using the Toggle Button

In this next example, we are going to use the **toggle button control** to investigate the **Timer Function**. A **toggle button** is used to indicate a state, such as Yes/No or a mode such as On/Off. The **toggle button** has a *Property* called *Value* that alternates (toggles) between *true* and *false* when it is clicked. The *Properties* default *initial condition* is *false*.

You can use the **toggle button** to hide and unhide rows, hide and unhide columns, hide and unhide a chart, switch between design mode and edit mode or as an alternative to check box. Either way you can see **toggle button** is very useful.

Allegheny Valley Institute of Technology ®

Authorized Training Programs

Exercise #7: Understanding the Timer Function

Open **Excel** and create the following **UserForm**:

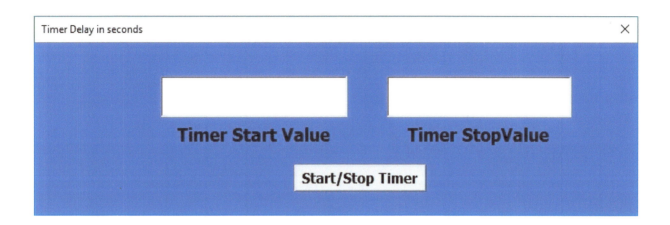

Save the workbook calling it **The Timer Function** as an **Excel Macro-Enabled** workbook.

The code behind the **Toggle Button** is:

```
Private Sub tgbStartStop_Click()
   If tgbStartStop = True Then
      txtStart.Value = Timer      'display the Start Value of the Timer
   Else
      txtStop.Value = Timer       'display the Stop Value of the Timer
    End If
End Sub
```

Use of the Timer Function to Time a Section of VBA Code

The following example shows how the **Timer** function can be used to time a section of **VBA** code.

```
' Time a section of VBA code using the Timer function

Dim secs1 As Single
Dim secs2 As Single

secs1 = Timer( )
' Code to be timed



   .

   .

   .



' End of code to be timed
secs2 = Timer( )

' Display the time difference in a MessageBox
MsgBox( "Time taken to run code:" & vbNewLine & secs2 - secs1 & " seconds" )
```

After running the above **VBA** code, the following message box is displayed:

File/Open   Loop Example 2
                     Find the time it takes to execute the **Do While** loop.

                     Then try: 100, 1000,10000 and 1000000.

Allegheny Valley Institute of Technology ®

Authorized Training Programs

Running Macros Automatically

You schedule **Excel** to run a procedure at periodic intervals or at a specific time of day, with the **OnTime Method**.

Using Excel's Application.OnTime Method

Use the **Application.OnTime Method** to run a procedure at specified intervals or at a specific time of day.

Syntax:

> **ApplicationObject .OnTime** (EarliestTime, ProcedureName, LatestTime, Schedule)

Using this method you can schedule to run a procedure in the future. You can either fix specific intervals, starting from now, when the procedure will run, or you can fix a specific time of day. The (**Excel**) **Application Object** represents the entire Excel application, and is the top-most object in the Excel object model. The **EarliestTime** and **ProcedureName** arguments are required to be specified while the other arguments are optional. The **EarliestTime** argument specifies the time when the procedure is to be run. The **ProcedureName** argument specifies the name of the procedure you want to be executed.

With the **LatestTime** argument you can set the time limit for running the procedure.
If you set the **LatestTime** to "**EarliestTime + 20**" and if meanwhile another procedure is being executed and **Excel** is not in ready mode within 20 seconds, this procedure will not run. Omitting the **LatestTime** argument will make **Excel** wait and run the procedure. Omitting the **Schedule** argument will default to True, which sets a new **Ontime** procedure. To cancel an existing **OnTime** procedure set earlier, specify **False**.

To fix specific intervals starting from now, to run the procedure, use "Now + TimeValue(time)".
To fix a specific time of day for the procedure to run, use "TimeValue(time)".
Refer to the following examples on how to use this method.

Allegheny Valley Institute of Technology ®

Authorized Training Programs

Stop or Cancel a Running Procedure (using the OnTime method)

If you attempt to close the workbook while a procedure is being run using Application.**Ontime**, **Excel** will re-open the workbook, and leave it open post completion of the procedure. Hence, you will need to cancel the procedure at a certain point or time.

To cancel a running procedure (using the **OnTime** method), the precise time of its scheduled run is required. Note that if you don't pass the time to a variable, **Excel** will not know which **OnTime** method to cancel, as Now + TimeValue("00:00:03") is not static, but becomes static when passed to a variable. This means that the time when the procedure is to run (EarliestTime argument) should be assigned to a variable (use a **Public** variable to make the variable available to all Procedures in all modules) and then use it to cancel the **OnTime**.

Remarks

- Use **Now + TimeValue(time)** to schedule something to be run when a specific amount of time (counting from now) has elapsed.

- Use **TimeValue(time)** to schedule something to be run a specific time.

- The values of *EarliestTime* and *LatestTime* are rounded to the closest second.

- Set *Schedule* to **false** to clear a procedure previously set with the same *Procedure* and *EarliestTime* values.

Examples

- This example runs the macro **Get Data** 15 seconds from now.
      Application.OnTime Now + TimeValue("00:00:15"), "Get Data"

- This example runs the macro **Open Valve** at 5 P.M.
      Application.OnTime TimeValue("17:00:00"), "Open Valve"

- This example cancels the **OnTime** setting from the previous example.
      Application.OnTime EarliestTime:=TimeValue("17:00:00"), _
      Procedure:="Open Valve", Schedule:=False

Allegheny Valley Institute of Technology ®
Authorized Training Programs

Using the OnTime Method in the AutoOpen Procedure

Exercise #8A

1. Place a copy of **OnTimeExample1** on your desktop and remove the read-only attribute.

2. Rename it: **OnTimeExample1A**

3. Open **OnTimeExample1A** and if necessary, **Enable Content** in the **Security Warning bar**.

4. Under the **Developer**, look at the **Module1** code window (3 macro procedures).

5. Change the "time parameters" in the **AutoOpen** procedure based on parameters given by the instructor. Then **Save and Close** the workbook.

6. Since the **AutoOpen** macro only runs the first time the workbook is open you must open the workbook again and wait!

Exercise #8B

1. Place a copy of **Loop Example3** on your desktop and remove the read-only attribute.

2. Rename it: **Loop Example3A**

3. Use the **OnTime Method** in the **AutoOpen** procedure to run the **DeleteRows** macro at a specific time and then use the **SaveExit** macro to save/exit the workbook.

Allegheny Valley Institute of Technology ®

Authorized Training Programs

Opening an Excel Workbook Automatically

Exercise #9   Using the Task Scheduler to open a Workbook

Task Scheduler

The **Task Scheduler** enables you to automatically perform routine tasks on a computer.

The **Task Scheduler** does this by monitoring whatever criteria you choose to initiate the tasks (referred to as triggers) and then executing the tasks when the criteria is met.

To run the **Task Scheduler**

Click the lower-left **Start button**, enter **schedule** in the empty box and select **Task Scheduler** from the results and the following screen will appear:

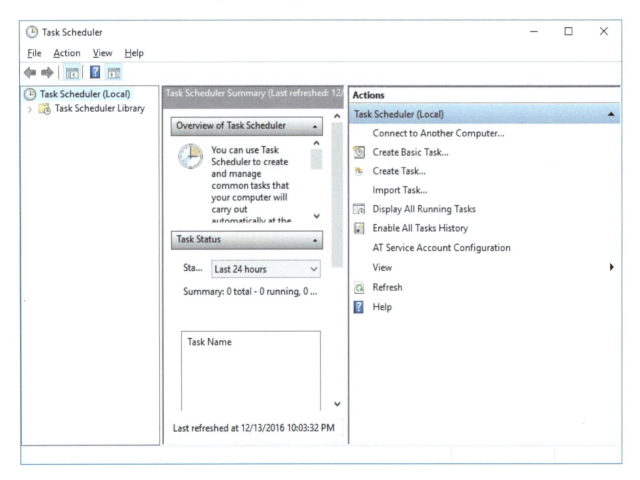

Allegheny Valley Institute of Technology ®

Authorized Training Programs

With the **Task Scheduler,** open:

1. **Create a Basic Task** called   Projects

2. Then click **Next**, schedule the task **One time** and click **Next** again.

3. Add 20 minutes to the present time and click **Next**.

4. **As an Action** choose **Start a program** and click **Next**.

5. In the **Program/script** field type: wscript.exe

6. In the **Add arguments(optional)** field, paste in the path to the file **Projects.vbs** and complete the path with the file name. Sample shown below:

        "C:\Users\Skip\Desktop\VBA Documents\Projects.vbs"

Yes, you need the path to be in *double quotes*!

7. Click **Next** and **Finish**.

8. Do not close the **Task Scheduler**. With the help of the instructor, manually test your task to make sure the vbscript code executes.

Wait for the instructor before continuing.

Editing the time to **trigger** the **Task Scheduler** task named **Projects** to run the **vbscript** to open the workbook.

9. Right-click **Projects** in the **Task Scheduler** and choose **Properties**.

10. On the **Triggers** tab click the **Edit** button and add 2 minutes to the present time.

11. Click **OK**, then **OK** and close the **Task Scheduler** and wait!

Yes, you can close the **Task Scheduler** and it will still launch the application!

Allegheny Valley Institute of Technology ®

Authorized Training Programs

How to use my **vbscript** file to open your **Excel** workbook:

Open **Projects.vbs** with **Notepad** and change its name to:

"your workbook name".vbs

Don't forget to change both the name and path to it!

Also, change the path to the **"your workbook name".vbs** in the *arguments* of wscript.exe in the **Task Triggers** properties tab.

Using Mathematical Functions in Formulas

Exercise #10   Building Equations in a Macro using Excel Functions

1st Button: Calculate the **Gain** based on the variables **Voltage In** and **Voltage Out**.

2nd Button: Calculate the **Hypotenuse** based on the variables **SideX** and **SideY**.

3rd Button: Calculate the **Power** based on the variables **voltage**, **current** and **angle**.

File/Open the workbook:

Mathematical Functions in Formula's for Students

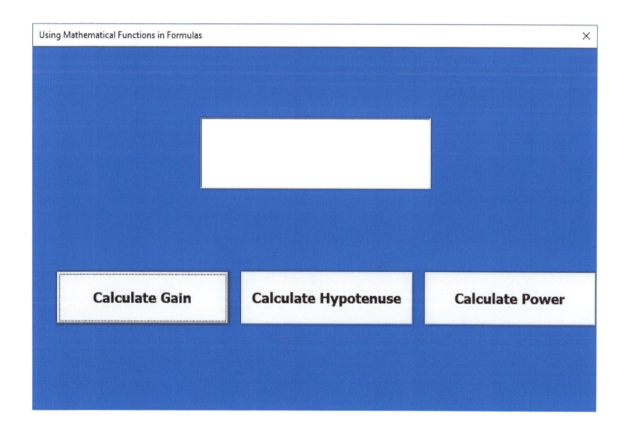

Allegheny Valley Institute of Technology ®

Authorized Training Programs

Notes for formulas:

Gain of an amplifier in **decibels:**

Hypotenuse of a right triangle in **feet:**

Power dissipated by an element in **watts:**

Working with Form Controls

When you interact with **Excel**, you do so through Excel's graphical user interface. A graphical user interface includes menus, dialog boxes, list boxes, scroll bars, buttons, and other graphical images called *Form Controls* or *objects*. A graphical user interface makes a program easier to learn and also helps reduce errors by restricting choices to valid options.

In the past, creating a graphical user interface has been difficult and reserved for professional programmers. More recently, advanced applications gave the ability to add graphical controls to custom dialog boxes. With **Excel** you can take advantage of dialog box-style controls directly on the worksheet, without doing any programming at all. In the following exercise you will not create macros, but you will become familiar with how to use *dialog box controls*. These controls can be very useful when designing **Full Application Macros**.

Exercise #11

Problem: We would like to create an easy to use worksheet that will calculate a car loan payment based on price, down payment, interest and years of loan.

Solution: Build a worksheet model to calculate a car loan payment amount.

First design a graphical user interface to make the worksheet model easy to use.

Before you begin, **File/Open**   CarLoanCalculator

Allegheny Valley Institute of Technology ®

Authorized Training Programs

Create the following worksheet:

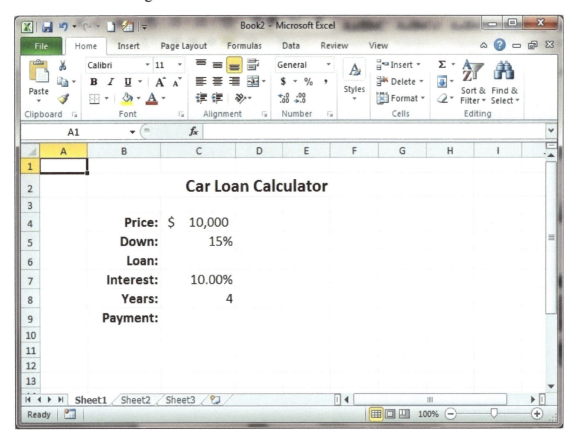

2. In cell C6 (to the right of Loan), type **=C4*(1-C5)** and press **ENTER**. The value 8500 appears in the cell.

3. In cell C9 (to the right of Payment), type **=PMT(C7/12,C8*12,C6)** and press **ENTER**. The payment amount **$215.58** appears in the cell. The red color text and the parentheses around the number in the worksheet indicates a negative number: the monthly payment amount.

4. Select cell C6 (to the right of Loan), and click the **Currency Style** button on the **Formatting** toolbar. Click twice on the **Decrease Decimal** button to show only dollars with no cents.

5. Select cell C7 (to the right of Interest), and click twice on the **Increase Decimal** button so that you can see fractional interest rates.

Allegheny Valley Institute of Technology ®

Authorized Training Programs

Excel has tools that enable you to create powerful user interfaces very easily. The user interface objects can help restrict entry options to valid choices, making your worksheet less likely to produce erroneous results, and easier to use.

Make a List for the Combo Box

1. Go to cell AA1, away from the main worksheet model, and type the follow table of cars:

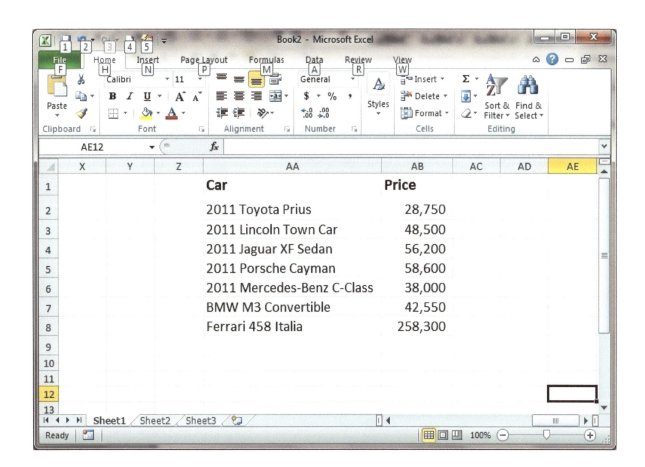

	Car	Price
1	Car	Price
2	2011 Toyota Prius	28,750
3	2011 Lincoln Town Car	48,500
4	2011 Jaguar XF Sedan	56,200
5	2011 Porsche Cayman	58,600
6	2011 Mercedes-Benz C-Class	38,000
7	BMW M3 Convertible	42,550
8	Ferrari 458 Italia	258,300

2. Select cell **AA1** through **AB8** to select the entire table.

Allegheny Valley Institute of Technology ®

Authorized Training Programs

3. From the **Formulas** tab, under the **Defined Names** group, click the **Create from Selection** button. Select the **Top row** check box, clear any other check boxes, and click **OK**.

This will give the name **Car** to the list of cars and the name **Price** to the list of prices.

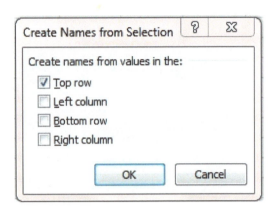

Placing Control Objects on the Worksheet

4. If the **Developer** tab is not available, display it.

   a) Click the **File** tab.

   b) Click **Options**, and then click the **Customize Ribbon** category.

   c) In the **Main Tabs** list, select the **Developer** check box, and then click **OK**.

5. Under the **Developer** tab, in the **Controls** group, click the **Insert** button.

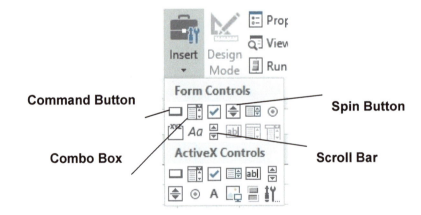

Allegheny Valley Institute of Technology ®
Authorized Training Programs

6. Click the **Combo Box** button and drag a rectangle from the top left corner of cell **E4** to the bottom right corner of cell **G4**.

7. Right-click the new combo box and click **Format Control** to display the **Format Control** dialog box, and select the **Control** tab.

8. Type **Car** in the **Input range** field, type **H4** in the **Cell link** field, and click **OK**.

9. Press **ESC** to deselect the combo box control.

10. Click the down arrow on the right of the drop-down control, and select **2011 Lincoln Town Car** from the list. The name for the **2011 Lincoln Town Car** appears in the drop-down control, and the number 2 appears in cell H4:

You have just created an on-screen combo box control. You linked the list box to the list of cars on the worksheet, and you linked the result of the list box to cell H4. Cell H4 displays the number 2 because the **2011 Lincoln Town Car** is item number 2 in the list.

11. To update the price from the list, select cell C4, type **=INDEX(Price, H4)** and press **ENTER**.

Restrict the down payment to valid values

1. Under the **Developer** tab, in the **Controls** group, click the **Insert** button. Click the **Spin** button under **Form Controls**.

2. Drag from the top left corner of cell D5 down to the bottom corner of cell D5.

3. Right-click the new **Spin** object and click **Format Control** to display the **Format Control** dialog box, and select the **Control** tab.

4. Type **20** in the **Maximum value** field and **H5** in the **Cell link** field, click **OK**.

5. Select cell **C5** and type **=H5/100** so that the down payment will be entered as a percentage.

Allegheny Valley Institute of Technology ®

Authorized Training Programs

Restrict the interest rate to valid values

1. Under the **Developer** tab, in the **Controls** group, click the **Insert** button. Click the **Scroll Bar** button under **Form Controls**.

2. Drag from the top left corner of cell D7 down to the bottom center of cell E7.

3. Right-click the new **Scroll Bar** object and click **Format Control** to display the **Format Control** dialog box, and select the **Control** tab and make the follow changes:

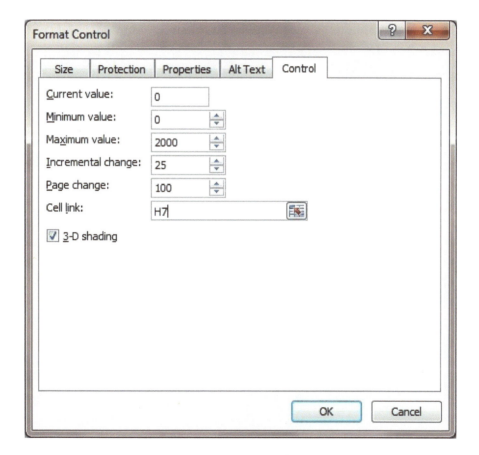

4. Select cell C7 and type   **=H7/10000**, and press **ENTER**.

Allegheny Valley Institute of Technology ®

Authorized Training Programs

Restrict the years to valid values

1. Under the **Developer** tab, in the **Controls** group, click the **Insert** button. Click the **Spin** button under **Form Controls**.

2. Drag from the top left corner of cell D8 down to the bottom corner of cell D8.

3. Right-click the new **Spin** object and click **Format Control** to display the **Format Control** dialog box, and select the **Control** tab.

4. Type **1** in the **Minimum value** field, type **6** in the **Maximum value** field and type **H8** in the **Cell Link** box, click **OK**.

5. Select cell C8 and type **=H8,** and press **ENTER**.

Allegheny Valley Institute of Technology ®
Authorized Training Programs

Centering Title and Removing Gridlines

After centering the title and removing the gridlines (under the **View** tab), your complete model worksheet should look like this:

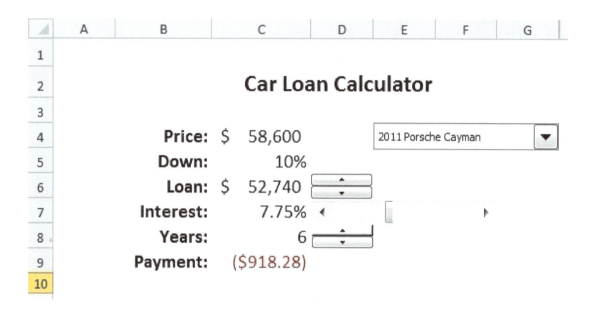

Final Issues with the Car Loan Calculator

The only remaining issues are:

- Unlock cells H4 through H8. (**Home/Cells/Format/Format Cells/Unlock**)
- Hide Columns H, AA and AB. (**Home/Cells/Format/Hide & Unhide**)
- Protect the worksheet (**Home/Cells/Format/Protect Sheet**)

These commands will be treated as a review. The instructor will step you through the steps to accomplish the above tasks.

EFL08/10/18

Allegheny Valley Institute of Technology ®

Authorized Training Programs